Imre Major, 48, father of two, is a Hungarian economist with a degree in law. During his professional career, he has worked mostly in the telecommunications, plastic processing, IT and automotive industries. He is usually referred to as the person who possesses the most pieces of irrelevant information.

Most of the time, Imre goes his own way independently of the expectations or against them. He tries to cope with the arising problems he causes himself and lives with the problems he causes others. After he has started to see the whole picture of human nature and more generally about life in an original way, he aims to deepen and share his understanding in specific fields.

This is his second book, exploring the sustainability context of the full picture. This time the goal is to enhance environmental understanding and more general sustainability aspects related to human nature and behaviour.

To my children, hoping that they will face their own challenges instead of the problems caused by the preceding generations.

Imre Major

THE BASIC ECONOMIC FRAMEWORK OF SUSTAINABILITY

AUSTIN MACAULEY PUBLISHERS®

LONDON • CAMBRIDGE • NEW YORK • SHARJAH

A CIP catalogue record for this title is available from the British Library.

ISBN 9781035876457 (Paperback)
ISBN 9781035876464 (ePub e-book)

www.austinmacauley.com

First Published 2024
Austin Macauley Publishers Ltd®
1 Canada Square
Canary Wharf
London
E14 5AA

Grateful to my parents, my brother, my four really good friends and their families who had or have been supporting me, and to my three teachers from secondary school for the really important lessons I could learn from them.

Table of Contents

Chapter I
Humankind in Its Environment

Main Questions Related to Environmental Limitations

One objective of Economics is to provide optimal resource usage, reaching maximum output for the given resources or defining the minimum resources needed for a given output. The question is if we sum up all these optimal resource usage do we get an optimal global resource usage? Is there an effect which leads to suboptimal activity by definition? What causes suboptimal resource usage, how we can evaluate the difference to the optimal usage, and how we can compare individual benefits to environmental changes?

What does sustainability mean? What happens in case our activity is not sustainable? Can we interpret sustainability on the level of individuals? Can we monetize environmental services similarly to human services available on the market? How technology changes alter our environmental evaluation? Are there solutions in case our economic establishment proves to be unsustainable?

These are the main questions I aim to resolve in this book, accompanied by sharing my understanding of sustainability.

Basics of Sustainability

We are part of our environment, we exploit it, we have an impact on it, we are depending on it, all these simultaneously and in a complex way. We cannot separate our activity from our environment, we cannot live without it. For sustainability, we need to reflect these links consciously if we do not want to excessively upset the balance. Understanding sustainability is to look for, see and interpret this balance in human terms. There are other types of balance we should consider, between our common and individual well-being and between our actual and future common well-being. It is not an easy task by any measures, looking for and considering signals from our environment and from our own societies can give us a lot of help.

Our natural environment is complex and huge, reacting with delay accordingly. It cannot easily tolerate overly rapid changes, despite our vast knowledge we are not fully aware of how life, our living and unanimated environment operates and we cannot follow all changes within it. Our existence, well-being and our economy are highly dependent on our environment and the services it offers. We constitute the social environment for each other, we depend on each other strongly as well, and human cooperation is a strong influencing economic factor.

We are deeply involved in our environment, our presence is heavily felt. Still, we cannot communicate with our environment, it has no centralized system, no leader, no knowledge library, no status report, no representative, and no bank account. We can negotiate only with ourselves and not with our natural environment, we cannot ask or persuade other species not to die out or not to spread when they are transported to new territories, and we cannot organise discussions between species to come to an agreement about the conditions on how they should live next to each other. Due to the lack of communication, other species accommodate and adapt to what surrounds them instead of what we want or what we agree on with each other. We can force other species to exist in an environment we create for them or to avoid our habitat however, this practice is limited and brings further changes beside or against our intention.

Providing an explanation or finding an excuse to maintain our unsustainable life will not save us, it would be similar in effect to finding an excuse to go extinct. There are always reasons to be found for any activity, and most of the reasons are valid. We can persuade or compensate each other for any external effect, we can force our will on each other and on our environment while it is much harder to evaluate the harm we do to the latter. Understanding the reasons why we are not acting sustainably helps us change our own behaviour but not in pushing further the environmental boundaries.

Sustainability is a complete and complex topic on its own. If the aspect of sustainability is connected to another question, like growth, profit or development, and they are discussed together, then that is a discipline of the connected phenomenon only which has nothing to do with sustainability.

The Missing Link Between the Human Race and Our Natural Environment

Our natural environment does not have a judicial personality, it has no lawyer, interpreter, social media account, or central office. When we negotiate with each other, and compensate an owner of an environmental body or territory for the harm we cause to them then it has a very indirect effect on the body or territory in question. The owner may or may not want to pay others to repair harm depending on personal thoughts, interest rate, concurring possibilities if there is any known way of repair and other circumstances. The environmental aspect is only one of many.

If we do not deeply understand our natural environment, if we do not care enough, if we do not take it into consideration during our business calculation processes, if we take its services for granted then we are losing environmental value, and mostly remain unaware of it for a lengthy period of time. When we cannot avoid seeing environmental effects, we name them as an externality and again we define how to compensate each other, not the environment. There are taxes levied on activities using or harming our environment however humans, companies or other man-made organizations pay to the state, involving the environment only indirectly if at all.

Globalisation Is a Fact

We are a global species, we are living and travelling all across the Earth, to high mountains, and deep seas, use land in many different ways, utilize all kinds of substances and create never before existing materials. The huge natural transport mechanisms and the effective mixing mechanisms in our environment spread our outputs globally, without asking or warning us. We humans mostly understand and obey territorial boundaries while our environment cannot interpret or be aware of boundaries between countries. Since we cannot persuade or teach other species or natural transport mechanisms about the meaning and importance of boundaries we should consider ourselves the boundary-less operation of our environment and we should think in global indicators, thresholds, and limitations accordingly.

We have all the tools to measure environmental indicators, communicate in this manner, share information, come to a common understanding and cooperate accordingly. However there is a strong contradiction between the particular interests and our common global interest, the next chapter is to shine light on these controversies and their origins.

Chapter II
Contradictions and Behavioural Elements Leading to an Unsustainable Economy

If Something Has to Give In, What Will You Choose?

If our activity consists of contradictory objectives and we pursue them simultaneously, something has to give in. As our lives and our economy are complex in most cases we cannot avoid harming someone's interest. The laws, expectations, our personal interest, the interest of other persons, organizations, groups, other stakeholders, and our environment can suffer harm without any bad intention from our side. Additionally, there might be a conflict between our personal interest and the interest of the group we are a member of, and furthermore between our actual and future interests. Other species, our natural and living environment have as well a complex network of interests. Most human stakeholders are protecting their own interests or fighting for it, articulating it, expecting it, buying it, and forcing it.

Additionally, our reputation, our income, our freedom or our life can be at stake if we cause too much harm to others.

The least resistance is offered by our natural environment, as it is not as organised as we humans are, it will not say a single word if we do something unsustainable to it. Unlike other role-players, who object in a short time and loudly when we harm their interest, the natural environment complies obediently, but not exactly the way we want. Furthermore, causing harm to our environment by taking resources from it is in many cases an advantageous process, usually the more resources are taken the bigger the reward is.

Generally, when a business activity does not rely on the human body or mental power only, it uses natural resources, thus due to the huge number of business actions the chance and extent to harm our natural environment are as well high. Due to the huge number of actions, by statistical probability alone we can cause a lot of harm to our environment, the least resistance of nature elevates the probability even more to harm other species.

Whatever business interaction we are dealing with, let it be barter business, buying and selling, or providing free services, we use resources, mostly natural environmental resources, and we clear account with each other and never with our natural environment. What we do to preserve our environment, to use less of its resources, is done very indirectly, the link is very weak. The environmental aspect is only one among many others.

In the modern economy, the value and income created have to cover the costs of investment needed for maintaining production, population, competitiveness, law and order, education, health, food, accommodation, and sustainability.

Furthermore, we strive for growth in many of these areas. The costs can rise strongly and there is no guarantee that the redistributed part of the created value and income can cover all these tasks. Additionally, the available budget is decreased by inefficiency, free-riders, corruption and the mafia. If something cannot be covered, in the short term the least visible item on this list is sustainability.

Daily Pyramid Building Games

Pyramid games have their own regularities. They show an attractive picture, but still, so far, they have never operated sustainably. The core of the pyramid game is that we put in money, or more generally, value, and we intend to take out more money or value from the inputs of the players joining after us. This sets a limit of growth in the long run, as the pyramid can go as high as new layers at the bottom can be laid. As there is absolutely no way to endlessly grow the bottom of the pyramid, the whole upside-down built structure will collapse as there is no stabilising mechanism present when the growing phase stops, the dynamic balance cannot be converted to a static one as the bottom layer becomes unsupported without further growth.

Many political or economic systems can be described this way. At the top of the pyramid, a lot of mouth-watering services await the fortunate ones, like power, dream job without the required education, huge income, extra high-level health services, expensive educational possibilities, person-targeted regulations, strong and direct influence on common topics and on other's life. The next level has spectacular services to offer as well, for example forming strongly audible opinions, excellent possibilities for self-marketing, high income without pertaining work, good educational and health services, and influencing position.

History has a lot of records of underserved careers, an overly strong influence on the lives of others, questionable incomes, exceptions, privileges, working around the law, and long-standing practices to cut curves. Pyramid games transfer value from a lot of people to a few, thus generating the otherwise hard-to-achieve wealth and power levels for the members of the top layers. In the beginning, the value input is barely perceivable as it is low at the following levels, while the reward at the top grows rapidly. The harm comes partially from the corrupted decision-making and lack of feedback. Being in a position without proper education, with limited liability only towards the upper level can lead to decision-making processes which do not take into consideration the personal interests of many stakeholders, the many people below the top, and who do not have the intention to accommodate to the circumstances and the environment the organization exists in, as it is not necessary from that point of view. The effects of such ignorant decision-making can be devastating, leading to waste, loss, slow reaction, further contra-selection, and unsustainable operation. The collective harm, despite barely noticeable on the personal level, is by orders of magnitude bigger than the sum of the rewards on the top.

It is not easy to do anything against pyramid games, even if we spot the concealed structure. Strong forces can be involved to pave their own way, it might be uncomfortable to stand up for something which is barely seen, at the beginning joining the party pays off much more than being left out and fighting it. If we join, we put in the value of supporting and maintaining the establishment, we surrender some of our possibilities to vindicate our rights and interests, and in return, we keep open the road to climb up to a height we otherwise could barely reach if at all.

The big reward is available for a short time only and on the top levels, still, in case of a large enough base, the structure can hold quite long. After some time, the cumulative harm and the corrupted structure grants reward to fewer and fewer people while the harm caused to others is getting more and more noticeable, later on becoming spectacular. All this results in imbalances, more situations allowing arbitrage, more and more bizarre techniques to maintain the actual order, and the growth of secret paths and person-targeted regulations. In the last period before the collapse, there is no reward except at the very top level, the structure bumps into limits and obstacles all the way, and the only personal goal is to get at least minimally acceptable services or to avoid punishment for normal behaviour. After that phase comes the collapse, the ruins cover everyone and everything, necessitating a long waste removal and restoration process, needing more resources and effort than the received payouts altogether.

It seems to resemble the way we are doing business and building the economic establishment within our natural environment. The base is huge, and rewards are paid at many levels close to the top, due to the population size of humanity we can maintain the pyramid building really long. Surrendering a little protection of our environment at our location, and not questioning the natural resource usage of others are the values we put in. Getting a lot of comfort, valuable products and services, secure life, and reliability are the rewards we take out. We already can see the deterioration, bizarre explanations appear as to why and how to keep up overusing of natural resources, and strange plans can be seen on how to avoid the most menacing consequences and still maintain and grow the comfort we are used to. Being left out is a less attractive possibility than squeezing out remaining values, and many role-players grew too strong to realistically step up against them, while the collapse of the establishment has not yet appeared on our horizon.

Being Free-Riders

There is a well-known phenomenon called the free-rider problem or the tragedy of the commons. In such cases, actually or in a more general way, the higher use of a given area or goods than what is sustainable or optimal in the long run ruins the area or goods. Time-wise usually this phenomenon occurs after a period of balanced use by further actors joining to exploit the commons, which at first yields more output with little harm to the common goods, however further joining deteriorates more rapidly the commons. The result is that the people who are using it above the optimal or sustainable level and who are looking for their own advantage only are losing the commons, just as everyone else. This phenomenon probably occurs more frequently than the occasions we explicitly label as the tragedy of the commons.

A common point in being a free-rider is that the person who is above the sustainable level of participants does not care about the risk to the common goods, and passively or actively deteriorates it even more, leaving the faith of the commons to its will to live or the intention of the others to maintain it and keep it usable and valuable. There might be several reasons to act in this manner, like being unaware, forced to do so, egoism, aggression, carelessness, and avenging being left out, but still, the result is the same. Additionally being a free-rider has deep biological roots. Being a predator, a parasite, or a virus all strongly resemble being a free-rider, living on resources used or piled up by others, deteriorating these and caring only to a level which is not harmful to the free-rider itself. Economic terms can be seen as a form of being a free rider, like cattle grazing in the common meadow, arbitrage, tax evasion, using support unduly, hacking, piracy, and bribery.

The free-rider strategy works mostly when the commons are big enough. One of the fastest ways to grow and advance is to use resources piled up or reserved by others, as the huge base of resource sources provides great power to redirect to the few free-riders and the huge base means long-time possibility without too much deterioration. Being a free-rider is a very rewarding strategy and there is no easy or natural way to prevent it as long as the commons are not ruined too much. In nature, we can see long-existing balanced states, among humans it is harder to achieve balance as there are more possibilities to become a free-rider, more technical ways to exploit common resources, more value to target, more rapid changes than in nature, more rewarding to use the piled up resources of others, and more conscious ways to pursue our personal interest. On the other hand, most of the protection methods, regulations, and threats for free riders are ineffective or cost more than the loss in the commons. Furthermore, it might be difficult to spot a free-rider situation, our nature does not set off warning signals, getting closer to collapse does not trigger any countermeasure, and there is no natural monitoring system.

Generally, every person who is living in an unsustainable way is a free-rider. The base of resources is huge, and the time till the deterioration becomes apparent is long, still if too many people follow the free-rider strategy for a too long time we risk that the truly common commons, our living natural environment cannot take such strong deterioration and collapses, killing most of the people and other species independently who was free-rider and who not. We are acting as free riders when we open an additional coal power plant, when we let more substances into our environment as before, and when we increase the energy need for more data, more service or more entertainment than before, without doing anything to get back to balance. There are many reasons why we think we cannot live in a sustainable manner, why it is not worth it, and why we do not want to stay off possibilities while others not, we can always find excuses, however, it does not make difference in the progression of environmental deterioration or the end result. From the aspect of sustainability, resource usage and balance matter.

Less Than the Total of Parts

It is a strong asset when something is more valuable than the sum of its parts. Equally, when the opposite happens it shows disruption, friction or lost efforts in the structure. Our global political-economic establishment seems to show marks of disruption, friction, counteracting efforts and fights. In 2023, we broke the all-time record for CO_2 output despite all the related pledges and undertakings and despite all the knowledge of the dangers and consequences of high carbon dioxide levels in the atmosphere. We face a growing global lack of manpower despite the rapidly growing global population. The number, efficiency and output of power generators running on renewable energy sources are growing exponentially, at the same time the number and output of coal-based power generators are soaring. The value we create, the availability of goods, and our comfort have never been so high, on the other hand, our world is becoming a more and more dangerous place, we face threats from each other, from other nations, from our environment. The value, capital and income accumulate extremely fast for the rich while the number of poor and the missing part of their income to live a healthy life are growing rapidly as well.

We are decades away from fusion energy production, promising limitless amounts of energy, but still, already they cannot cover the unlimited electricity hunger of artificial intelligence, cloud services, crypto-coin mining, data storing and other information technology services. Artificial intelligence was created in mind to prove solutions to yet unanswered challenges, however, this technology now creates hard-to-answer threats to a menacing extent. Solitude is growing despite the many communication channels available. The growth of expectations outpaces the growth of possibilities in the fields of work, education, leisure, and online presence. The growth of human knowledge and scientific progress are unstoppable, still, we see fights and wars based on more and more primordial, tribal, primitive conflicts. The level of international cooperation is dropping despite the available communication channels, business relations and personal connections, and the growing need for cooperation. The more we use antibiotics the less effective they become.

The sum of particular interests does not necessarily equal the interest of the whole species. The previous is closer to the interest of the political-economic establishment, still the interest of the pronounced goals like free market, democracy, hearing and supporting oppositions, freedom of choice, creating value, development, growth, profit, lessening dependency, enhancing scientific knowledge, creating efficient tools to achieve these goals, is not in direct correlation with the interest of the human race, which is survival, with sustainability being an essential tool for it.

An important question from the aspect of sustainability is the border between private business and common affairs. How do the many personal needs become common interests? If something affects us or harms our personal interest, what is the process to make it a common question? Answering incorrectly this set of questions can threaten sustainability severely.

Advertising and Sponsoring

Advertising and sponsoring are valid, powerful and in many cases helpful economic tools with effects well beyond the economy. Advertising is drawing attention mostly to a product, a service, a company, an industry branch, a behaviour, an idea or a case with the intention to raise demand and thus sell more services or products at a higher price. From an economic point of view if the cost is smaller than the extra revenue, then advertising is justified. Typically it is not a question if the advertised product, service, company or activity is sustainable or unsustainable, the primary decision point is whether the expected yield is higher than the cost or not. More or less generally the companies and organizations with high marketing budgets are the ones whose activity involves heavy use of environmental resources.

The same applies to sponsoring with the added effect that the sponsoring is evaluated more to be successful if the created attention is higher, as a side effect resulting in higher environmental resource consumption for the sponsored event. From a sustainability point of view, a harmful case is when a company heavily involved in the overuse of natural resources sponsors an event which uses a lot of environmental resources and attracts a lot of people, who need more environmental resources, in return generating more demand for the resource burdening product or service. The company is in the positive range with their cost covered and their public perception elevated, the audience participating in an event otherwise unaffordable, and a lot of resources are spent for comfort and joy, all these at the expense of our natural environment. The yields are tangible and spectacular in the short term, while the harm caused to our natural environment is much less visible. In the long term, this evaluation turns to the opposite. On the other hand, there is no way to sponsor our natural environment. Furthermore, losing our biggest and long-time sponsor, our natural environment would be disastrous.

A great contributor to advertising is our ego. The target of many commercials, our ego is the persuading force that makes us believe all the shiny messages. And it is the same ego that does not let us become satisfied, maintaining our desire to buy new products and services again and again despite having met our needs already. And our ego is the hurdle in evaluating our activities reasonably by overriding our thinking and self-reflection. For doing business, our ever-hungry ego is a reliable and strong driving force, while it is at least as strong a hindering force in reaching sustainability and it makes our life more difficult in many other ways.

Our ego makes cooperation and objective evaluation more difficult. Besides our ego, another contributor to the success of advertisements is our constant desire to excel and stand out from the others, as if we were constantly in the mating season. We are similar to other species in the way how our level of aggression and jealousy rises during mating season, and unlike other species, we have little to no breaks or calm periods between mating seasons. We create extra demand by our desire to stand out, burdening our environmental resources, while on the other hand, we burn extra bodily, mental and creative resources.

Control over Supply Chains and Sales Channels

Many companies and entities consider the control over the supply and distribution chain to be a criterion of sustainable operation, still, this control and its effect on sustainability are limited. The market demand, which the companies strive to meet is mostly out of their control, the higher the demand is the more natural resources are needed, independently of the control of the company. Demand is not in direct correlation with sustainability.

In many cases, the first step, the production of the raw material is achieved necessarily by technologies which deteriorate the natural resource during production. On the other end, the control over the distribution channel ends with the consumer, who does not necessarily consider environmental impacts during the application of the product or when getting rid of it. Probably there is no way to achieve and maintain control over the whole supply chain or the full sales channel. Furthermore, this type of control has no impact on the demand, which can lead to sustainability issues if it is overly high. A manageable level of demand could strongly contribute to sustainability.

We Create Too Much Value

Since the Industrial Revolution and thanks to the economic processes advancing since then free time and free income are available for more and more people. One important result of modern times is that they are available simultaneously. In consumption-based societies, there are many ways to spend both, there is no special need to look for possibilities, choosing between them in the close to unmanageable amount of advertisement and other sources of information seems to be more difficult.

There are beneficial industries based on our leisure spending. Transporting people, conducting attractive programs, providing food, offering personal services, and creating luxurious conditions, all provide a boost for the local economy and create further income to be spent. The supply side has a lot of advantages if managed right. The demand is pushed further by the more and more mentally demanding modern economy, the high-stress levels which need to be counterbalanced, and the achieved free time and disposable income are primarily serving this goal.

On the other hand, building up, maintaining and developing the infrastructure for transporting people, goods and information, the limits to regulate the people involved is a considerable environmental burden. Additionally due to local weather seasonality, holiday and vacation schedules or regular closing of big factories mean peaks in the demand, and a constant or hard-to-change infrastructure must meet these occasional demands which lead to even higher resource demand and unused capacities for long periods.

As the disposable income grows, so does the demand, the high prices become regular, the luxurious services become expected by the masses, and the resource needs as well go up accordingly. Demand creates supply, in case of conflict between the demand to spend time and money and the environmental impact in most cases the environmental aspect will give in. Additionally, due to global processes like atmospheric and oceanic circulations, the dimensions of our environment and its absorbing capacity, the environmental impact usually appears somewhere else or sometime later, breaking the direct link between the usage of natural resources and its effect. Becoming a free-rider of this type is an attractive alternative, especially in the strong competition on the market.

As the level of values increases, inevitably so does the level of complexity of our life. New technologies, new regulations, new customs, new rhythm, changing mediums, context and content of communication, higher amount of knowledge to be learnt and less available time for it, all these lead to elevated stress levels and reduced accommodating possibilities.

As free time and disposable income can be converted to other types of value, the amount of value we create is getting higher, to the level where the too-high value creates its own risks. The items of value get more complicated with modern technology. Too high values are harder to protect, it can be too attractive to become a free-rider, to take share unduly from someone else's value. Furthermore, with the advances of technology, the amount of available tools to get hold of a value is increasing while the protective measures are getting more complicated, thus needing more resources. Acquiring value with delinquency is getting less risky, hiding the identity of the involved actors is getting easier, and having to face personal punishment is becoming less likely.

The increasing number of possibilities to spend time and money has its drawbacks. More media content is created that can be reasonably perceived, even without assessing its credibility. The rapidly increasing number of mind-altering substances in order to counteract the growing stress levels is leading to losses of very personal resources. The huge demand for these substances, which creates the supply, leads to desperate fights for the power generated by this demand, fights and groups overwhelming state monopoly on applying military forces. Additionally, the companies to meet the increasing demands for energy, goods, services, information, and entertainment are coming to an unmanageable size, possessing much more resources than the states and organizations which should regulate them. The overly high level of values leads to unmanageable conditions in many fields.

We assume that if we gain more money then we will be more satisfied and will have more tools to protect our wealth. While these assumptions might be not fully true, they partially explain our never-ending monetary dissatisfaction, leading to a widening gap between rich and poor, and they provide a reason for the resistance to prioritizing sustainability.

Roles with Impact on Environmental Resources

There is a deep gap between the benefits of those who use natural resources and the efforts of those who intend to protect natural resources. For a for-profit organization, growth is one of the most rewarding changes, generating revenue is part of the core activities, using natural resources is the normal way of operation, and the profit is enjoyed by the few owners. For a non-profit organization, growth means increasing costs, generating income is a task which takes resources away from the core activities, and reducing or redistributing resources in a non-economic way is the objective while the results are enjoyed by other people.

The business model to use environmental resources usually incorporates efficient methods to call and influence the targeted consumers, the tools are mostly available for those who can cover the cost of using these beneficial marketing tools, which suggests high usage of natural resources. Those who are not affected directly and immediately by the deterioration of natural resources have an easy path to exploit to a high extent the available natural resources. In most cases, those who have the tools to reach many people are not interested in other than advertising their own goods and services, regardless of the intention, talent, or thought on the environment of the involved people, it is purely coming from the role.

Who has the intention to call people to protect natural resources without the financial and economic background originating in the use of natural resources has limited means to reach its goals. The same applies to companies and organisations who lost their powerful background due to the deterioration of the used natural resources, in case they want to warn or persuade others to avoid similar failure, they have lost their efficient communication tool to reach enough people together with the used natural resources.

There is no role in our societies or among the international entities, which has simultaneously the power, authority, intention, and tools to efficiently influence others to avoid the overuse of natural resources. Some of them possess the power or the tools however they face strong limitations. Some see fewer restrictions while they lack the power or the means.

Humans have the right to the highest level of health, which is mostly secured by adequate environmental circumstances. In case we lack these circumstances, we hold each other accountable, we settle the related economic and legal disputes within humanity, which means an indirect link only between the activity which deteriorates the level of natural service and the impact. There is no legislation or global limitation for interactions between humanity and its natural environment. Additionally what we do not measure remains unknown, our environment does not spoil us with information about itself, nor does it force us to measure the environmental parameters or hints on the parameters to measure. We cannot start direct negotiations with nature or settle in a financial way the human usage of natural resources. We lack direct contact thus the only remaining tool is the indirect way, however, its efficiency is limited.

Lawmakers, legislative and law enforcing authorities can create and apply laws however they can regulate anything in detail only after a technology or a phenomenon becomes apparent. The area is limited by the border, and the power to enforce the law can be limited in many ways and by many circumstances. The complexity of the modern economy and natural environment, and especially their changes are happening on a higher frequency than the speed level legislation can operate on. Additionally, the natural environment has no representative or articulated interest, the operation of an entity and its impact is mostly separated in space and time. Generally, the complexity and lack of knowledge regarding our natural environment have very little in common with the way of legal thinking, the logical structure, the related information in advance about thresholds and sanctions, the clear distinctions and limits, and the threat of punishment for those who disobey the law. For jurists, our natural environment is a given state, an external endowment, a facility with little to do with it.

The members of the scientific community have a lot to say about our environment, the transparency of their research, the repeatability of their experiments, their methods to measure environmental parameters, their reliable and proven models, and their understanding provides strong contribution to protect environmental resources. On the other hand, their well-grounded limitation to act outside science, their self-restriction in political topics, and the lack of economic, legal and political power leave communication as their only tool.

What they tell us however means only one source of information among many others, and likely to be the first one to be omitted as it serves general interest only, not the particular interest of the ones who have economic, legal or political power.

Politicians have powerful tools in their hands, moreover, their main tool of operation is power. Their role is important and a lot depends on the correct work and understanding of the politicians on local, state, regional, international and global level. Still, politicians are representing the interest of those who vote them into power and keep them there which means a strong limitation by itself. Nature has no representative and thus has no vote, and no politician can pursue the goal of protecting natural resources against the interest of voters and affected companies and organizations who live on the usage of natural resources. If a politician harms the interest of a group that keeps him or her in power in a short time, the said politician loses his or her main tool of operation. A politician can represent the need to protect natural resources only when the majority of the voters want it. Due to the size of nature, and the thus arising belated impact, when the majority of the voters and those who keep the politician in power require the protection of natural resources, it is likely too late to effectively protect these resources from deterioration.

Furthermore, the planning horizon is below the time period needed to have a presentable effect on the environmental resource which needs protection. The politicians for international organizations are aware of the limits of their responsibilities and tools. Generally, the more voters are behind a politician the more power he or she has, on the other hand more voters mean more contradicting interests to represent at the same time, which in turn means a less pronounced goal of protecting natural resources.

Military forces are powerful, sometimes their presence or existence is enough to make others obey. However environmental aspects are among the very last points on the importance list of the heads of the armies, environmental related goals come into play only if there is a fight for income generating or basic resources, like land area, mines or water sources. History shows that there are more and stronger arguments at hand to start a war than to avoid conflict in order to protect environmental resources.

Consumers and consumer groups want to consume and do that with ease. The general state of the environment and availability of resources do not resonate well with their specific demands. The intention of the consumers is more related to the price, availability and content of the goods and services, not the environmental circumstances. If the deterioration of natural resources affects the availability of goods and services, in most cases they have a direct replacement therefore deterioration of natural resources impacts consumers indirectly and with delay.

Climate-protecting activists and non-profit organizations have limited resources to persuade and influence others, their main tools are the sharing of knowledge and information, a strong will to achieve their goals, and communication with being on the spectacular and loud side as an efficiency-improving tool. In the case of direct activities, the achievable goal is limited by the resources at hand.

The right to exploit natural resources can be more or less limited by regulation, the actual possibility is open to everyone. The benefits are enjoyed by many, the price is paid by many, the question is the correlation between these two groups. The actual trend is that the number of benefactors is dropping, and the number of price payers is rising in parallel to the change in the proportion of rich and poor people. The disparity of access to natural resources is growing, and doing it at an accelerating pace. The delay of the natural environment in effects following human economic-political impacts means that in the foreseeable future, the benefits of exploiting natural resources will serve fewer and fewer people while the deterioration of natural resources will be felt by more and more.

On the individual level, lacking a similar extent of organisation as the business entities, there is not much we can do. Living more passively, staying off of something that is useful, advantageous or comfortable, albeit harmful in any way to our environment, can be beneficial for ourselves and our local environment, still this way we cannot contribute to global sustainability. On the other hand, harming locally our environment in a spectacular fashion is nowhere near the common, industrial type deteriorating our global political-economic establishment imposes on our natural environment, we just lose our personal justification to stand for other species or to call off business entities that harm our environment on a more industrial scale.

A sign of an unsustainable way of life is when the different roles get into a conflict of interest. We should consider the level of unsustainable practice to be higher when the same persons by switching roles can get into a conflict of interest with themselves.

The Power of Separation

One of the great tools humanity got hold of shortly before and during the Industrial Revolution was separation. Famous experiments and scientific results like Dmitri Ivanovich Mendeleev's clear separation of elements, Gregor Johann Mendel's great understanding of genetics by concentrating on a single genetic variable, Sir Isaac Newton's separation of white light into its elements and all his scientific work far advancing his time, all these had led to effective scientific research, efficient engineering and applying goal-oriented technologies. Science has changed from long or lucky, sometimes smart observations to direct research looking for answers to a single point or a small set of questions.

This way of thinking has found its way into economic science and business practice, partially by studying only a single or a small circle of elements and more importantly providing tools to achieve single objectives. These can be goals like profit, growth, bigger market share, retaining workforce, creating a desired perception about the company or the organization, building influencing power, and supporting others, however, these are separate goals and though they can lead one to another they can be achieved simultaneously with strong limitations. Sustainability cannot be broken down into stand-alone parts which when achieved separately would mean sustainability per se. Additionally, environmental sustainability and long-term business success are both goals requiring complex planning and constant accommodation, which are achievable by no known and easy means, and it is hard to aim for both as they are not aligning objectives, to say the least.

There are always at least one or a few single points of aspect which have better alternatives. On the other hand, we can always fund counterarguments for a solution based on a single part or a few single points which are better than the proposed ones. In our complex environment, we can hardly find Pareto optimal changes. If we aim for sustainability, we need to look at the complete settings, establishments or solutions to compare them as we cannot mix subsystems, or separated points, creating never before existed freaks or impossible combinations and taking them as a basis for comparison.

The term ceteris paribus, or assuming everything else remains the same, has limited validity in our complex economy and even more in a complex environment. Our common thinking is closer to concentrating on a singular part and assuming at the same time that changing it has no impact on anything else. If we want to reach sustainability, we need to move our thinking closer to complex evaluation and planning to match the complexity of our natural environment.

The Power of Being Organised Within the Largest Joint Stock Company

If we look at the living species in the world as members of a joint stock company, we can find many particular interests, mainly existence, a lot of groups with common interests, groups with conflicting interests, internal links, and a lot of impact on each other, and all these changing with time. One species stands out in an aspect, namely being organised, it is the human race. Thanks to our big brains, communication, planning skills, cooperation, research, gathering knowledge, sharing memories and plans, and ample use of technology our impact on other species is orders of magnitude higher than of any other species, and higher than it would be justified by the size of our population, body size, biomass, speed, strength, robustness, capacity of self-healing, or other biological property. We are the species with the highest spread, still which is not the reason alone for such a high impact on other species.

Being organised and cooperating on a deep level means that we can access many more types of resources in much higher amounts than we could if we did all the needed steps individually and summed the results at the end. Using technology adds a lot to our common capabilities, allowing us to pile up resources, widen technology, distribute resources and transfer them to other types of resources. Technology means the capability and the act of changing our environment. The use of technology, together with piling up and transforming resources has a huge impact on our environment, including other species.

While our impact on others and the whole company is huge, we are the only species sending representatives to the managing board. This disparity leads to a mismatch between our capabilities to make forcing decisions favouring our particular interests while we are not taking responsibility for the whole company, the task arising from the same position. Due to the lack of communication with other species and the lack of representatives of other shareholders, we cannot delegate responsibility. Instead of looking at the interest of the whole company, like maintaining complexity, protecting environmental value, taking into consideration the internal links and particular interests of other species, and ultimately the existence of as many species as possible, the members of the board are looking more closely at the activities of the other member of the board and intending to counter them to their own benefit.

We can take our own body as an analogue. The number of our body cells is in the comparable range with the number of bacteria living in and on our bodies. Our body cells are operating in an organised, harmonious way, while we cannot communicate with our bacteria, they communicate only with each other very little if at all. The consciousness and the decision-making is ours, as well as the freedom to choose our activity and change the environment we live to a certain extent. Still, we are highly dependent on our bacteria, their population, and the links among and between them, without their presence and their well-being our own existence would be in danger.

The value of the company can be defined as the sum of the contributions of the stockholders. An important part of the contributions is the link between the species, their population, and their activity. Additionally, the harm caused to each other can reduce the common value, just as the dependencies on each other have the same decreasing effect. Too much or too strong dependencies bear the risk that if the supporting species cannot provide the elementary services needed for survival or the supporting species goes extinct, it takes away the resources from the dependent species which cannot substitute supporters in the available short time.

With only humanity represented on the management board, we are maximizing and optimizing the services needed by groups and entities within humanity, without enough consideration of other species' dependencies and their resources. For us, it is beneficial in the short term, the price of which is paid by the dropping value of the whole company in the long run.

In case we are not assessing correctly the risk of dependencies, then we are not protecting ourselves by protecting our supporting species. The same applies to our unanimated environment. With our advanced technology, we can replace one dependency with another one, separately we see solutions for many single dependencies. The free market is effective because the dependencies are close to imperceptible thanks to the many close-to-equal players. In any other type of economy, the difficulties arise from the more pronounced and noticeable dependencies. Still, in our complex environment, we cannot avoid considering the complete network of dependencies without risking our survival.

Breaking Logical Chains

There are logical chains in connection with sustainability which is easy to see, still, we are prone to break these chains at one link or another. Breaking a chain does not have a direct consequence like breaking the law in a well-controlled field and getting fined, still, it leads to false accommodation to the changes in our natural or social environment, or to not accommodating at all.

There is no alternative or spare environment, we cannot ask for a less polluted one, we cannot force warranty rights for a sturdier environment, there is no shop of new species nor can we resurrect any by viewing more ads. If we do not protect our natural environment, including but not limited to resources we use and we might use in the future if we let it deteriorate or if we harm it ourselves, we endanger our business, our comfort, and our existence.

The human race is the species with the highest spread on Earth. We are a global species, we are linked together with distribution, commerce, tourism, the internet, social media, and standardisation. The effects of these are accompanied by migrating species and atmospheric and oceanic circulation. The results of our activities add up, cover the globe and have an impact on all of us. We are in strong co-dependency with each other and we are depending on other species and natural resources as well. If we want to be in security, we should be careful not to slip out of this network or not to harm this safety net.

A rewarding type of business model is to rely on natural resources. As the demand is not limited by finite resources, the more resources used the more rewarding for the business entity. Due to the size, the supply-limiting effect of the deterioration of the natural resources comes into play with a delay. Everyone has the possibility to use our natural environment, and if someone can present a minimally reasonable cause, like consumer demand or doing good business, gains the right to use natural resources. Using and deteriorating our environment is not spectacular in many cases or it can be veiled to the level that it remains under our threshold. Regulations aim to limit activities locally and ensure local safety. The harms accumulate, independently of human borders, and reach around the globe, creating tension between locally beneficial activities and global safety, and furthermore between the locally enforceable regulations and the global impacts. Generally, we choose the reward for our activities and do less to protect our environmental resources.

Our environment is huge, which means any activity is affecting it with a certain delay. We can benefit from this delay as it opens the possibility to maintain for a longer time the business model relying on natural resources which thus can be perceived in the short term to be limitless. It hinders the need to accommodate the finite nature of resources, thus the necessity to seek sustainable business models. Furthermore, in case we want to take back all the harm we inflict on our natural environment our restoration activities will take at least the same amount of time to have an effect, assuming applying the same or similar technology and utilizing the same level of organisation as the actual political-economic establishment provides. Assuming exponential growth, as we see in most cases since the Industrial Revolution, the costs caused by the deteriorating environment, or alternatively the cost needed to restore the natural resources to a previous state, are also growing exponentially, just with a delay. It is easy to calculate the extra cost with each year of delay in starting to aim for sustainability, still, it seems as if we relied more on the miracle of technology than on common sense. More efficient technology can shorten restoration time, being not so organised and conducting the restoration activities with less effort, fewer resources and less enthusiasm as doing good business before, can lengthen the healing process. Still, it seems that we want to enjoy this delay to its full extent.

Due to the delay, our dependencies can grow with the deterioration of our supporters. The grace period caused by this delay can be converted to financial results instead of coming up with sustainable business models. If we start to counteract our harming activity when we see the impact, our countermeasures will have their effect delayed as well. It means we want to overcome challenges increasing in gravity and in number with fewer and fewer tools available, especially if we step over tipping points. In that case, a further deterioration leads to orders of magnitude higher impact in a short period of time. Seemingly, we are facing the risk of stepping over tipping points fearlessly.

If we encounter a problem, one solution is to push it outside of our direct and close environment. If we need fresh air, we let it into our room from outside. We use an air conditioner to cool air next to us and push the excess heat, plus the additional heat coming from the AC unit, to the outside of our home, our workplace or our vehicle. We like to charge our mobile phones and vehicles at our workplace. We place our garbage just outside of the border of our home or transport it via sea freight to the other side of the globe to be processed. Companies are doing the same, they cannot avoid doing so. They are using resources and creating substances and energy they do not want and neither can store at their own premises forever. Atmospheric and oceanic circulation take these away, and other species eat them up, transport and transform them. The companies cannot reasonably reduce their resource usage without losing their capability to compete with other companies. We are a species with high spread, we apply powerful technology, and as long as sustainability is not our number one priority, this pushing out of material and energy sums up and covers the whole Earth, coming back to us in one form or another. On the global scale, there is no outside.

We Accommodate Falsely

We are accommodating and adapting falsely when the driving force behind them is not sustainability. The tools to achieve sustainability are taking into consideration the natural resources we depend on, understanding the link between them, and acting responsibly and in accordance with our position within the natural environment. Our actual political-economic establishment seems not to consider sustainability as the number one priority.

When we train our body, we run, we jog, we lift weights, we swim, we do push-ups with the goal of keeping our body in shape then we are accommodating to our past. Our survival in the present rarely depends directly on our ability to run, jog, swim fast or for a long time, lift heavy weights, to achieve a high number of push-ups. Living a long life only partially depends on being fit, our survival relies more on capabilities like tolerating stress, constantly learning, meeting expectations, and being continuously alert and available. Furthermore, our lives and survival depend even more on how we can manage our technology, how we can defend ourselves against misusing or harming the technology we depend on, and how we can advance our technology in a way that does not lead to challenges we cannot answer. Probably we are the only species which has to accommodate its past instead of its presence and can do it without the high and direct risk of going extinct.

By watching series and television screenplays, where we are free to watch them at our own pace and they do not necessarily require our active involvement, usually, we are seeking relaxation and entertainment. Series mostly present a unique, never happened or once-in-a-lifetime situation or happening, otherwise they would present a lower entertainment value and we would be less interested in watching them. Additionally, these series and screenplays are usually attractive as they are spectacular or easy to understand. One of the main advanced functions of our brain is to help us survive, working for it our brain memorizes dangerous scenes, gathers, compares and processes information, and uses tools like empathy and planning to draw up escape or fight plans for different situations we see others get in. Due to the uniqueness of the seen scenes and situations, we will never get in, despite we consciously know the rarity, impossibility or improbability of the seen situation, still our brain takes everything at face value and processes the misleading information, burdening counter-intuitively our memory and our imagination.

We already overload our conscience with thousands of decisions to be taken, and a lot of information to be learnt and used which are far from the environmental conditions and biological happenings our brain accommodated to process mostly automatically. Burdening it more with irrelevant information our brain is far from relaxing, leading to a long-lasting conflict between our actual experience and what we train our mind for. Feeding our brains with more unusable information can confuse our brains. The same applies to being hooked on social media. We are prone to show mostly our best side, which creates a mismatch in perceiving the nice and shiny life of those who we know and what we see with our naked eye in our surroundings, confusing our brain. This self-strengthening cycle of conflicting experience and imagination can lead to growing numbers of mental disorders, accompanied by the stress caused by the processed and ultra-processed food we eat instead of the raw or minimally processed food our body is accustomed to.

Books and theatre scenes are somewhat different in this regard despite being similar in many aims. They are meant to teach us by making frequent but not so unambiguous situations clear, while they rely less on being spectacular and more on our active involvement and reception, we cannot read too fast a book and the pace of a scene in the theatre is set independently of us, thus we cannot binge-watch them as we do with the series. We can more or less solve this false accommodation of our body by training our body as if we were still in the environment of our past, however, we cannot do the same with our mind and we do not want the same with our food, mostly due to comfort and to economic reasons. Generally, our body and our mind are accommodated to more physical challenges and fewer mental tasks, with our mind supporting our survival with several automatic processes. Our lives change more rapidly than our bodies and our minds can accommodate to the more technology-based, more cooperation, more decisions to be made and more stress tolerance requiring way of life.

Many are great supporters of free markets and do business as if they worked on really free markets, with equal access to raw materials, knowledge and information, without limitation. Theory and practice can be different in this regard. The markets seem to be restricted by political influence, state support and customs, taxes, military threats including restrictions on double-use products, corruption, overwhelming bureaucracy, mafia and hacker activities. The truly interchangeable standardised products have a low count and strong desire for differentiation bringing emotions into decision making to the cost of conscious data-driven calculations.

We are regulating our business life and common activities to a high extent, mostly concentrating on relations and interactions between humans. We do it in a complex natural environment, without accommodating to or getting known to the regulating mechanisms of our living environment. As a result, we set our sights low, short-term interests override long-term goals, and measurable business results weigh in more important than sustainability.

We accommodate falsely and have no chance to survive if we, instead of aiming for sustainability, settle for accommodation in the changed environment. Our environment does not go to another unpleasant, albeit fixed state, but changes more rapidly and to more extreme values. The rapidly changing environment, which is an erratically moving target in itself we want to hit, can move to parameters which are out of our reach of accommodation or adaptation. More importantly, the species we depend on cannot accommodate the drastic and erratic changes, especially as the changes come in rapid succession, we cannot protect them if we are concentrating only on our own direct survival.

Do We Have an Objective?

In our actual state and trend which do not seem to be sustainable, can we infer to any purpose, any objective which is worth making our future life difficult or impossible? Besides comfort and fulfilling the never-ending wishes of our ego, is there any reasonable goal we chase that can justify the unsustainable production, consumption and use of our environment? Like safer living conditions, being protected from our harsh environment? The advance of technology, development, whatever might it mean? Consumption, consuming more than yesterday or consuming more than others? Maintaining a competitive market or competition itself? These can be goals however the unsustainable way we live turned them back. On a personal level, we are more secure, more comfortable, have access to more advanced technologies, we can consume endlessly, we can compete in fields of our own choice, all these to a higher level than ever. Our common safety and comfort are declining, technology is getting to the threatening realms and our common consumption is less and less attractive. With all the values that are hard to protect and with increasing international tension, we cannot be secure from each other either.

Any particular or personal long-term goals can be read out from our economic behaviour, or do we have only short-term goals? Without any apparent elevated or sublime idea these most clearly articulated goals seem to endanger our long-term survival. Can we muster at least a single long-term objective that is not cut under by the effects of the short-term goals? What economic output, what level of comfort and luxury or which growth rate makes acceptable the risk of becoming extinct?

Being safe from the harsh environment has been desired practically since well before the human race appeared. Being safe from each other ditto. We have been seeking comfort all the time. However due to a mismatch between optimal resource usage for particular interests and goals and globally optimized resource usage, added with the consequence of the not sustainable practices, our unorganized short-term goals counteract any given global objective and make the lack of the said objective more and more threatening on the individual level. The too rapid changing of our environment, induced by economic necessities and excess demand, directly risks our safety, our comfort, our business model and our existence. Without sustainability, every other objective loses meaning.

Chapter III
Definition and Theory of
Sustainability

Defining Sustainability

Natural resource means the capability, act, material, energy or service of our natural environment which humankind has the capability to exploit or actually exploit. These can be raw material; energy in the form of electromagnetic wave, radioactivity, heat, kinetic, motional, or chemical energy; capabilities of absorption, renewal, restoring, healing, balancing, or accommodating; transforming, transferring materials; being reliable while bearing variation; physical space, habitats and spaces containing life, spaces free of human-generated noise, vibration, light, smoke, smell, disturbing materials.

Some examples of resources: plastic-free environment, free orbital space, light pollution-free night sky, electromagnetic wave and radioactivity free environment, not counting radiations coming from natural sources, radiation-free freshly molten iron and steel, the level of complexity of practically any habitat, less time needed for other species to accommodate or adapt to changes in their respective environment, an environment free of everlasting chemicals. Some of these resources cannot be restored to their original state, the question is how we can live with that, or which other resources need to be restored more deeply to counteract the loss of these resources? Alternatively, what should we do till we develop technology to restore the seemingly unrestorable resources or work around them?

There are human-induced changes we probably can never reverse, like non-natural level nuclear radiation, creating deserts on the land or in the oceans, driving species to extinction. There are changes with very long reverse periods like clearing the skies from the satellites and getting rid of the residues of plastics, forever chemicals, and composite materials. There are substances we dumped into our natural environment for so long and in such big quantities that normalizing their levels needs huge efforts and a lot of other resources.

We need to consider nature's tools like complexity, variance, will of life, accommodation, adaptation, and intelligence. There are a lot of links, context and constant changes we are not or we cannot be aware of. We need to consider the time needed for other species to accommodate and adapt to their changed environment. It is easier to ruin something than to restore it, decreasing the value of a natural resource is faster and easier than increasing it. The natural environment and other species can help us if we let them.

Life on Earth is complex and contains a lot of dependencies and different types of dependencies. Species can be dependent on each other, and live in co-dependency, the dependency can be one-way, bidirectional or circular, and shorter or longer chains can exist. Species generally depend on the broader environment as well. We humans are no exception, while we have greater freedom in choosing and transferring our dependencies, still we depend on natural resources. Sustainability means that we do not make life harder or impossible for the species we depend on and we do not deteriorate the state of the unanimated natural resources we depend on. In other words, we do not decrease the value of our natural resources.

Probably the human race is the first one to have a long-standing and deep consciousness and level of organization that had such a strong impact on the supporting species and unanimated resources. Previous to us, and especially to the Industrial Revolution, sustainability was close to self-evident. Now we have the knowledge, technology and power to move toward individual survival. If we do not use the same knowledge, technology and power to advance sustainability our common and individual survival gets endangered. Technology means the capability and the act of changing our environment. Viewing from the aspect of species and resources we rely on sustainability incorporates their modification as well, thus we have to act with care not to change too rapidly, too strongly or too harmfully the supporters in our chain of dependency. Sustainability means human acts and human-induced changes do not increase the number and strength of dependencies nor do worsen the conditions of the supporters we depend on.

This definition lets us see the consequences of unsustainable practice. Making the possibilities and circumstances worse for the species and unanimated environment we are depending on means we create deeper or new dependencies we have to answer with fewer and fewer tools available at hand. It is possible to reply to the thus arising challenges to a certain extent however it bears the risk that at a point we run into unsolvable problems. Unsolvable problems mean loss of available tools or technology, habitable territory, species or material we are directly depending on, loss of human lives, and finally extinction. Additionally, it is more difficult to advance a saving technology amid higher stakes and under bigger pressure.

Defining Externalities

Externality means the difference perceived by humans between the levels of exploited services offered by our natural environment, where the difference is caused by direct and visible natural links, following each other in the chain of dependencies. The difference is used to be cleared between humans depending on the value, however, it is important to note that the difference may be orders of magnitude smaller than the value of the other natural services we exploit.

By extending the scheme of externalities to other species and for longer sections of the dependency chains with more links, we can enhance our understanding of sustainability. What happens between other species shows a striking similarity to externality, of course without the financial clearing of the differences. The idea that the circumstances of our supporter, its well-being, and the change in its situation affect us is an important aspect of sustainability.

Primary and Secondary Products

Our machines and structures run on resources, and energy sources, and produce outputs, transformed energy and substances. Additionally, they have some functions which are useful for us, we create these machines with the purpose that they serve their humanly intended goal. We cannot replace our natural environment or buy another one, there is no spare environment, therefore, we have to consider the outputs and the consumption of energy and material as primary functions and the intended functions as secondary ones as we can live without moving ourselves for fun, on risky high speeds or with insane acceleration, moving half of the world's goods for cost saving while on the other hand, we cannot live for long with a deteriorated environment.

If we create an oven and burn oil in it, it produces substances like fumes, ashes, gases, small particles, and energy like heat, sound, light, and vibration. These are primary products. If we mount wheels or wings on this oven or build a ship around them, the primary products remain the same, however, we gain secondary products like transport, travel, heating systems, and night lights. If we load tubes with explosives or rapidly burning materials, we get similar primary outputs. We get secondary products like fire rockets for entertainment, for killing other people, for lifting objects in the sky and above.

We can create woven materials from glass, carbon or plastic, we can coat them with resin or reinforce them with plastic, we can form them into delicate shapes, make them easy to work with, we receive durable, lightweight materials. For secondary functions, these are advantageous properties, for sustainability, the durability can cause more problems as there is not much we can do with these materials to dismount, dissolve or reasonably get rid of them. We can create substances that last long and are effective in killing species we evaluate as harmful. These are secondary effects, with the primary impact of accumulating in other species as well throughout the food chain due to the long lifetime of these substances, haunting us at the top of the food chain for long periods. A step toward sustainability could be to keep in mind the primary products and effects when we design the level of efficiency and lifetime while we aim for the secondary products and effects. Less efficient and long-lasting tools, substances and impacts could mean more sustainable primary products.

We provide reasons to produce primary products like we need the secondary products for the comfort, profitability, efficiency, safety, and luxury they offer. In business calculations, we consider mostly the secondary products and we expect from advances in technology to reduce the needed quantity of primary products to obtain the desired secondary products. From the aspect of sustainability, only primary products matter and the above reasons should be evaluated more as excuses.

Extended Demand-Supply Graph

The Demand-Supply graph shows the demand and the supply in one diagram as a function of quantity and price, with the horizontal axis showing the quantity and the vertical axis the price. The supplied quantity goes up with the price while the demanded quantity goes down as the price goes up. Their crossing point presents the market price on a free market. The shapes of the demand and supply curves vary from market to market. What is missing is the limitation of available resources and the ends of the lines presenting supply and demand further away from the balance point, as we are prone to end the lines abruptly as they are getting close to the axes.

The situation closer to the truth is that the long end of the lines are nearly parallel to the pertaining axis as above a certain wealth, when the demand is not in correlation with the price, it remains close to constant at any price level and supply is neither limited due to the relatively low volume. Above a certain wealth, the disposable income is perceived as infinite, stepping out of the realm of the basic assumption of Economics, namely the scarcity of resources. Still, this is a considerable demand which creates its supply and from the viewpoint of sustainability, we have to take it into account. This consumption which misses most of its rational basis is generating a huge demand in needed resources thus strongly and unnecessarily burdening the available natural resources.

The curves have an economic, which means a human, origin, with only very little connection to the available natural resources if at all. It is not a realistic objective to achieve sustainability if we place the market demand above the scarcity of natural resources or we consider only the demand generated on the market. The graph will present more precisely the consumption if we draw the demand and supply curves all along, till their realistic endpoint. As full information is not always obtainable about the demand for every price point or to have good enough resolution it is still important to estimate the curve. The quantities summed, that means the area beneath the lower part of the curves, the curve of supply till the crossing point and the curve of demand after that, represents consumption, which we need to compare with the sustainable level of resource supply. From the resources needed for the given product, we should take the scarcest one which gives the lowest supply for the given product.

As sustainability can be interpreted on a global level only, we need to sum the consumptions of all local markets or at least about the ones which generate the major part of the global demand and compare it to the global resource supply which does not lead to a drop in the value of natural resources. The global resource supply should be considered only by quantity as the aspect of sustainability cannot interpret prices. To have a clear picture if our global economic establishment is sustainable or not, we should do this summing for all natural resources which provide supply for all consumed goods and services. Probably, at the actual state and in the next decades the precision of this summing cannot be realistically expected. Still, by rerouting efforts and resources from strongly resource-consuming, albeit not necessarily needed for survival activities, we can come up with a relatively good and usable estimation. Alternatively applying a certain safety margin to a relatively low global consumption can be a good starting point, considering the lack of information and feedback from the consumption groups like armies, private military forces, mafia, and grey and black market players. The global level and the safety margin should be regularly updated to see if the global consumption meets the global natural resource supply, whether it is over or remains under, decreasing or not the value of the natural resource in question.

The intended effect of advertising, namely selling more products or services for a higher price, is working in the opposite direction than the environmental limitation introduced in the Demand-Supply graph. It is possible that a well-conducted marketing activity is justified from the economic point of view as it yields more return than its cost, still from the aspect of sustainability advertising can be justified only if the demand elevated by advertising remains below the sustainable level.

Summing Optimized Local Resource Usage

From the practical side, partial knowledge or better to say the incompleteness of the Demand-Supply graph leads to suboptimal global resource usage, resulting in the overuse of natural resources. Theoretically, optimal resource usage can mean optimizing the output from the available resources or calculating the minimally needed resources for a required output. Assuming optimal resource usage in every single case, summing the local optimized usages and for the different types of resources, we can achieve global sustainability only in the case of everyone always choosing optimization of the output from the available resources. On a local or individual level, we see that we can freely choose between demand or supply-based optimization of resource usage. On a global level, only supply-constrained optimization is sustainable. If anyone chooses to order the needed resources in an optimal way for a required output, then sustainability is harmed.

Sustainability shows similarity to how money changes over time. We can convert actual money or value to future money or value while we have to consider the interest rate or calculate the expected growth. Similarly, we can borrow future money, including the calculation with the interest. When we are acting in an unsustainable way, we are borrowing value from our future. Sustainability means we decrease the interest rate to zero or close to zero, however, in this case, we are doing nothing to pay back the capital, the previously accumulated burden of materials, energies, broken links and changes we have introduced to our environment, we are just not deteriorating our environment further. If we are placing our bets on technology, which equals interest rate decreasing even into becoming negative that is a possibility. Still in this case we have to calculate the changing demand, which can result in higher consumption leading to an altogether higher resource usage from the less resource burdening technology. Another possibility is direct capital payback by reducing our production, environmental input and output below the needed level of sustainability.

We have a word for sustainability, but still, it means only that we do not deteriorate the environment we are dependent on. There is no word for making our position better as our thinking is not revolving around it, nor has it been an objective during our long history.

Measuring the Unfathomable

It is not self-evident how we can measure the value of services offered by our natural environment. If we take the market value, if a market exists at all for the given product or service, the value is determined by market movements much more than the value or state of the environmental resource. Furthermore, our knowledge of the natural environment is limited, not even counting the constant and rapid changes in our environment, including human-induced changes.

By evaluating human interference with nature, we need to consider that due to our powerful technology, we can introduce changes to our natural environment so rapidly that other species cannot accommodate or adapt to their new environment. The links between species and the unanimated environment are complex and delicate, it is orders of magnitude easier to reduce the number of links than to increase them, and it is much easier to weaken the accommodating or adapting capability of a species than to strengthen it. For these reasons, it is much easier to reduce the stress tolerance, and pollution absorbing capability of a species, even if we take special care towards them, thus reducing the value of an environmental service by human interference is close to self-evident, we can look at any global human impact on our natural environment as being harmful and devaluating by default. There might be minor deviances, they will not alter the big picture though.

A way to define the value received from our living environment is to compare the actual state of the resource with the most valuable and most complex state, namely free of human intervention, and to sum the needed efforts and resources to get back to that state. To connect the value of environmental resources to perceived values we need to estimate how much human effort, and how many resources are needed to restore them to their original state. The value of a natural resource can be defined as the distance from the original state expressed by the cost of efforts and resources needed for restoring the original state, and change in the state of a resource can be calculated as the difference between the two states' distance to the original state, or equivalently as the needed effort and resource to get back to the previous state in case of relatively minor changes. Due to our limited knowledge firstly we can estimate roughly the order of magnitude of the needed efforts and resources. If we want more precise evaluation, we need to spend more effort on gaining knowledge and monitoring the parameters of our natural environment. The value of a natural resource or service is not fixed, it can change over time as technology advances, thus lessening the needed efforts or resources, or we lose a technology due to resources becoming unavailable, and natural changes can lead to changes in the evaluation by helping or hindering us in restoring the original complexity.

We can define the value of the services of our natural environment if we look at and concentrate on natural resources on a global scale. We can do this as we are a global species with global impact, and how we affect our globe is completed by the global transport systems of nature, like migrating species, and oceanic and atmospheric circulation. We can disregard smaller, local impacts as they are felt locally and countermeasures can be taken as well locally, the needed efforts and resources to counteract the impacts can be summed with relative ease.

If we are within sustainability, the already-used economic laws can work and rule our lives. Technology offers the possibility to elevate the strong limitation on demand, additionally, our changing environment can alleviate our task if we are lucky. On the other hand, if we lose technology or our environment deteriorates, we have to reduce demand, production, consumption or output further, accommodating to the new state of technology or to the changed environment. We need to constantly monitor our environment and adjust our economy accordingly.

In case we deny understanding the value of services offered by our natural environment, if we consider only the market value and we think that we cannot create a link between the value of the natural resources and the value defined by the market we are risking to loss environmental value at a high speed and to the extent where restoring the state free of human intervention becomes impossible at more and more natural domains.

We Seem to Be in Reverse Gear

Due to the immense difference in how strongly and rapidly we can destroy links in our natural environment and how slowly we can restore them, with the addition of the strong governance of market value over the value of the services offered by our natural environment, together with the human ego and limited knowledge, can lead to situations where we misunderstand and misconduct our behaviour from the aspect of sustainability.

Our political-economic establishment rewards those who act for themselves, on the other hand, makes life harder for those who are active for their environment. Similarly, more resources are allocated to research and developments which can be converted to an increase in income or market value, to contrary environmental and sustainability-related research.

Economy and to some extent politics are ruled and directed by human needs, biological and psychological needs and desires, which are only in indirect connection with our natural environment. We negotiate with ourselves and not with our environment or with other species. On the other hand, we depend strongly on our natural environment and we cannot communicate with our environment, including other species. The way we organize our life and business is the opposite of the direction of our dependency, and we discuss with each other what to do with our environment, and how to exploit it, instead of looking at the state and condition of our environment.

We rule in a complex way what is a private matter and how it can be influenced by third parties. From the aspect of sustainability, everything is private matter what is sustainable, and solving all unsustainable issues is a common interest. Individuals, organizations or business entities agreeing on exploiting natural resources are interested in doing good business or meeting demand by exploiting more and more resources and thus are interested in keeping their business a private matter. The involved parties usually are doing business with due diligence, obeying laws, correctly clearing accounts with each other, paying taxes, and providing salaries for the workers. Still, sustainability should be the deciding factor if it is a private or common matter.

The above contradictions between the rules of our political-economic establishment and the sustainability conditions lead to our current practice where we do harm more to our natural environment and depreciate resources on an industrial level, more rapidly and deeper than stated in the wildest conspiracy theories. We disrupt societies and groups more rapidly than they could form and get established. Ideas, ideologies, and human conflicts rule political thinking and discourse, instead of sustainability and the logical decisions originating in the need to preserve the value of natural resources. Questions that need to be discussed together, voted on or chosen a path for a long time are less numerous than the number of debates and quarrels we actually live in. This way our common life would be much easier to understand and interpret, furthermore to cope with the less rapid changes would be an easier task, for other species as well.

As the species with the highest impact on our environment and other species, our responsibility is undeniable in choosing a common way of life or an establishment in which we strive to maintain sustainability, complexity, value of natural resources or not, whatever might be our objective or excuse. Exploiting natural resources without ensuring to do it in a sustainable way might be good for us individually, however, it is less good for other species we rely on and depend on, and ultimately not good for us as a species.

The difference between accommodation and adaptation is that in the case of a changing environment in the first case, the organization in question changes itself or its behaviour to survive, in the latter, it changes its environment to survive. Adaptation is similar to technology with the additional aim to survive, technology itself is a tool to change our environment. As humanity mostly lost its capability to change its own organism and is reluctant to change its behaviour, we mostly rely on adaptation. Furthermore, we are prone to pursue technological advances without any connection to survival. Still, if we want to aim for sustainability, we need more accommodation and less adaptation, achieved by mostly changing our behaviour consciously. More environmental accommodation and less business adaptation would bring us closer to long-term survival than the opposite way.

It seems that anything we do counteracts sustainability even if we act with the objective of getting closer to sustainability. The known and used economic rules and links should be obeyed within this framework, not considering the environment we live in leads to unsustainable practice. In case it is not the number one priority and we do not see the basic links and context of sustainability, if we do not mirror them in our economic framework, we have no chance to achieve sustainability.

Chapter IV
Limitations

Conflicts, Fights and Wars

In case we think whatever difference, contradiction or tension is the main ruler of our life, as if every other aspect would be a closed case and we can redirect our resources to resolve that conflict, let it be ideological, political, religious, sexual, tribal, national, ethnic antagonym, or originating from the clash of human egos, from sustainability aspect the order of importance is the opposite. Many resources are directed to express our identity, our religion, our political stand, our personality, and our sexuality, to protect these against other's influence, or to impose our ideas and expectations on others. As long as all sustainability issues are not solved every other conflict is aggravating the problems arising from conducting an unsustainable economic practice. The parties in conflict are in most cases equivocal partners in overconsumption and waste of resources, concentrating efforts on solving conflicts which are less important from the sustainability aspect. Considering sustainability issues as solved and concentrating on other disputes can lead to a self-strengthening cycle of resource-based conflicts, leading to more and more harm caused to each other and to the common environment, imposing hard-to-forget insults and injuries to each other and accumulating environmental pollution to a higher extent than the actual economic needs explain. Non-sustainability issues can lead to conflicts and fights to the extent that so many resources are wasted that a basic fight for the remaining resources can occur.

War and military conflicts are impossible to interpret from the sustainability aspect. The resources needed to develop, manufacture, maintain and use weapons are unproportionally huge, while the objective of the weapons is to annihilate, destroy or render useless or unavailable the resources of the target, or to strip the target from its accommodating or adapting capability. Every step of creating and using weapons is strongly against sustainability, even without considering the race of arms, when building up an arsenal of weapons and counter-weapons is inevitable to maintain balance, spending enormous resources just because the other party has spent enormous resources on weapons. Furthermore, among weapons' objectives, sustainability is not present as it would reduce their designated effect. We cannot reasonably expect armies or lawmakers to seriously consider the sustainability aspect as it would mean risking becoming vulnerable against others who disregard sustainability and build and maintain strong and effective weaponry. All these mean we would need to consider reaching sustainability by preserving natural resources more at other branches to compensate for the unsustainable nature of armies, and additionally others who disregard sustainability, or we need to decrease the number of existing weapons simultaneously and in a controlled and transparent manner in order not to disrupt the balance of military power.

The Task of Understanding Our Environment and Our Economy Within It

So far, our knowledge of the aspect of sustainability related to our natural environment has been limited. A possible series of tasks would be to build up an object-related, far-reaching monitoring system to follow the global environmental parameters on as many measurement points as is reasonable. Additionally, active and deep research should be conducted to understand the dependency links and chains of other species and to see the dynamics and changes.

Similarly understanding our past is missing, a related task would be to rethink our economic history through the glasses of sustainability and evaluation of natural resources to see what price we have paid so far for all advancements, safety, comfort and luxury by losing environmental value. Without understanding our history we risk making the same mistakes again.

An ongoing task would be to maintain global communication and transparency, without it, our task to act globally would be harder. The alternative would be to not to change our actual practice of changing our environment rapidly, till our circumstances, the deterioration of our natural environment forces us to act globally, in this case, the question would be if we were in time to act due to the delay caused by the size of the environment.

Common Understanding and Global Actions Are Needed

The topic of sustainability is broader than economics. It is more about common human behaviour, thinking, understanding and acting. Still, Economics is a vital part of it. This work defines the basic frame around Economics similarly as our environment encircles humankind, we need to mirror this situation consciously. My work serves the purpose of understanding our dependent position on our environment and its services, our position among and above the other species. There are basic laws, requirements and contexts of sustainability, if we want to aim for sustainability, we need to reflect these in our political-economic establishment. This book is serving this mirroring purpose, without hinting at any practical solution on how to reach sustainability, and this work only suggests where we should place it in our priority list. If we frankly want to achieve sustainability, then we need to conduct global discussions and to come to a common standpoint, and after that to act in an organized, harmonized, transparent and regularly realigned way.

Probably there are more solutions to reach sustainability. Still, if there was an easy solution we could find it as we have had plenty of time for it. The actual political-economic establishment, in which I do not want to point to any actual governance form or country, is more part of the problem than the solution, as, in case of any conflict of interest, the set of natural and environmental interests regularly takes the position below political and economic sets of interest. Any government, political or economic body which is not open to global communication, to step up together with other actors for sustainability, to take common actions, is moving further away from sustainability. Practising an unsustainable way of life is a global problem, we can solve it only together. Going further on the actual way, not changing our behaviour but our environment instead is not viable in the long run.

The scope of this work is not to provide a solution but to help understand why our global economy shows symptoms of being unsustainable. Still, independently of understanding how we can achieve sustainability, either as described in this book or another way, for a possible solution please refer to my book 'Our Inherently Controversial Human Nature – and How We Should Hack It' published by Austin Macauley Publishers in 2023. Please read it for a deeper understanding of our human nature, to see a viable alternative, which involves global thinking, understanding and acting, to have a picture if there is a long-term objective, which might help us in achieving sustainability.